"An Insp Calls" A* Guide From ACE Notes

DES JONES

ACE Notes Guide to achieving an A* with "An Inspector Calls"

"An Inspector Calls" is one of many long used texts for G.C.S.E. exams and Controlled Assessments. It's a tightly plotted play with clear themes, representative characters and social comment - this is why the book has proved to be perennially popular with students, teachers and examiners. It is also a rich source of ideas for analysis which can impress examiners and force them to place your work in the highest bands of assessment.

The aim of this revision resource is to give you the tools and ideas to achieve an A grade or preferably an A* grade in responses to the text of "An Inspector Calls". If you are capable of a C grade, you can use some of the following tips and analysis points to manoeuver your exam answers into the very top grades.

As a successful Head of English in a London comprehensive school, the details I will give you have been tried, tested and proved to be highly successful in guiding students to the top for many years. It must be emphasised that there is no magic formula to make you cruise to success with no effort – the aim of this resource is to put you in the position where you can create your own success.

In this resource you will find:

- Consideration of J. B Priestley's intentions for the play and the effect it would have upon his audiences.
- Discussion on why the author created each character - what did each character contribute to the message which the author wanted to put across?
- Analysis of Arthur Birling?
- Analysis of Sybil Birling?
- Analysis of Sheila Birling?
- Analysis of Eric Birling?
- Analysis of Gerald Croft?
- Analysis of Inspector Goole?
- Analysis of Eva Smith?
- Analysis of Edna?
- What is the significance of when the play is set?
- What is the significance of where the play is set?
- Suggestions for essay/answer planning
- Model introductions to essays on the novel
- Detailed sample essay plans
- Useful targeted quotes

The aim of this booklet

The key approach for those students aiming for the higher grades is breadth and depth of analysis. That is to say we don't just comment on the story and its characters but we spend most of our time considering the implications of the story, characters and action.

One of the main interests of examiners over the past few years is the candidates' ability to recognise and comment on author's voice. In other words, they want you to explain and evaluate what message you think the author was trying to put across to his/ her readers. Throughout this booklet, you will be given some ideas on what the author's intentions may have been thereby enabling you to travel along the A* path of analysis.

Consideration of J. B. Priestley's intentions for the play and the effect it would have upon his audience.

As a well known socialist, J.B.Priestley was concerned with the lives and wellbeing of ordinary people. British society had changed a lot since the First World War but Priestley still felt that there was a long way to go to achieve fairness for everybody. He felt that the rich and powerful exploited working people in order to maintain their own positions of wealth and influence. In order to draw attention to this, he set "An Inspector Calls" in 1912 rather than in the 1940s when it was actually written because before the Great War, the British class system was at its strongest and its unfairness was at its most obvious. Through the older Birlings, Priestley wanted to show his audience what he saw as the corrupting influence of power and wealth. It was clear that there had been some movement away from the rigid class system which had controlled Britain before the First World War but Priestley felt that the change had not been enough and had taken far too long to change a small amount. The still existent class system in Britain of the 1940 was seen by Priestley as selfish, unfair at the expense of honest working people and corrupt to the point of criminality. For these reasons, Priestley wanted to portray it in its worst form and for this, he created the Birling family.

In common with most writers of substance, J. B. Priestley realised the power of words and knew that the more people saw his play, the more his ideas about society would be put before the population. His aim was more than realised as the play proved to be his most popular work at the time and during the intervening years.

Add your own notes here:

Discussion on why the author created each character - what did each character contribute to the message which the author wanted to put across?

Priestley's characters are very carefully drawn in order to put his ideas across and the crafting ranges from the near caricature of Arthur Birling to the more complicated messages conveyed by Eric. Between them, the characters represent Priestley's views on the contemporary British society as well as his hopes and fears for the future.

So, now we can move on to consider Priestley's aims and intentions when crafting the characters and plot of "An Inspector Calls".

Arthur Birling

If any character could be considered to be the villain of the play, it is Arthur Birling. Representing the successful middle class, there is very little to empathise with in Arthur and indeed, Priestley wants it this way. Birling has already been rewarded by the corrupt section of society which he aspires to by being made a Justice of the Peace and Mayor of Brumley. He is a staunch "party man" yet despite his slavish support for his wealthy and privileged betters, they still look down upon him much like he looks down on those below him. This can be evidenced by the fact that Gerald Croft's parents are not present at the engagement celebration for their son and Sheila Birling.

Arthur has no compassion or feeling for other people – he is only concerned with his own advancement. Even the lives of his own children take second place to his selfish pursuit of his own ambitions. He is complacent in his own success and confident of his own importance. Priestley sets out to destroy any respect the audience might feel for Birling's achievements by having Birling make statements and predictions which the audience would see were glaringly and blatantly wrong. One of the clearest examples of this is that the Titanic was "absolutely unsinkable".

What is the point of Arthur Birling?

He represents all that Priestley thinks is wrong in British society. He wants to cover up what he and his family have done but only because it could affect his own advancement. He learns nothing from the Inspector's visit and we can see at the end that he will never change. Priestley's message of hope is that it is the younger generation who will change things for the better once the dinosaurs of Birling's generation have died off.

Sybil Birling

The perfect foil for her husband, Sybil Birling exists to protect the wealth and privilege of which she is a part. She sees her role as to protect her family, not emotionally or morally but in terms of reputation regardless of whether they are right or not. Priestley uses the character of Sybil to forcefully illustrate the hypocrisy of her class – she chairs the charity group but refuses to give the required assistance which the group is supposed to exist for.

What is the point of Sybil Birling?

Arguably even more unpleasant than her husband, Sybil Birling shows the audience that the older generation of the ruling class are unsaveable and underlines Priestley's belief that the only hope for the future is the social education of the younger generation.

Sheila Birling

At the start of the play, Sheila is presented as a shallow and self-centred product of her upbringing and class. She is only focused on the fairy-tale engagement between herself and Gerald and thinks nothing of ruining an ordinary girl like Eva Smith on a whim. Like her brother, Sheila's initial selfishness is a direct product of her upbringing and perhaps we can't blame her for her behaviour at the beginning.

Almost as soon as she comes into contact with the Inspector, Sheila begins to change for the better as she realises that all he actions have consequences for someone and she and the Inspector are the two most positive characters in the play.

What is the point of Sheila Birling?

She shows that there is a possibility of change for the better as she realises the error of her ways. Until the Inspector arrives, Sheila has only the role models of her parents to base her behaviour on and acts accordingly. The Inspector educates Sheila in Priestley's theme that we are all responsible for the effects that our actions have upon others.

Eric Birling

An immature young drunkard at the beginning of the play, the character of Eric behaves exactly as he has been brought up to behave by his parents and his class. However, as he sees the consequences of his actions, Eric grows up somewhat and we realise that the Inspector's visit has been an education for Eric. This education is one of social responsibility as opposed to the approach to life he has learned from his parents.

What is the point of Eric Birling?

Eric turns out to be a positive character by the end of the play as we believe he has learned his lesson and will lead a more responsible life in the future. Importantly, Eric has seen through the hypocrisy of his class and will be a positive instrument o change.

Gerald Croft

Like Sheila and Eric, Gerald is a product of the class system, brought up to believe that what he wants is important above the needs of those considered to be inferior to him. In his favour, he looks after Eva Smith or Daisy Renton a she was known then, giving her what she herself says is the best time of her life. However, once Gerald has had enough of Daisy, he dispenses with her showing no regard to what will happen to her in the future. Gerald is somewhat older than Sheila and Eric and although he could be said to have a foot in both camps, it seems that Priestley sees him as more a part of the 'old guard' who cannot have a positive influence on the future as Priestley sees it.

What is the point of Gerald Croft?

Unlike Sheila and Eric, Gerald is already too set in his ways to change. Although he shows some compassion in his treatment of Eva Smith/ Daisy Renton, he is still a product of his class and reverts back to normal once he finds out that the Inspector is not genuine.

Inspector Goole

Priestley makes no secret of his admiration for Inspector Goole describing his presence as 'massive' and giving great emphasis and weight to his pronouncements. Goole cuts through the hypocrisy and bluster of Birling showing him for what he is – a self-serving and corrupt coward who is clearly not fit for the position and influence which British society allows him. The Inspector is portrayed as a fair minded man who gives all of his interviewees a chance to redeem themselves but he is unmoving on the moral rights and wrongs.

What is the point of Inspector Goole?

He is the catalyst which brings together all the themes of the play and forcibly presents the moral position to the audience. From his portrayal, we must conclude that the Inspector is the voice of a higher moral authority and his other worldliness gives his pronouncements more impact than an ordinary Inspector might project. Therefore the Inspector is intended to be the voice of honesty and morality or, indeed, the voice of the author.

Eva Smith

The character we hear about but never see, Eva Smith is the embodiment of what Priestley saw as the oppressed majority of British society. When she tries to make things better, her modest attempts are thwarted by the self-interest and hypocrisy of the decaying system which is in place to control her and those like her; the system of course represented by Arthur and Sheila Birling.

Eva Smith could be any working person and Priestley wants his audience to sympathise and empathise with her plight in the hope that this will lead to the process of change for what he saw as a rotten and divisive system.

What is the point of Eva Smith?

Eva is intended by Priestley to represent all working people who Priestley saw as potential victims of their rulers' greed. As a young, personable woman, she is non-threatening and very easy to sympathise and empathise with. Thus, Priestley makes the actions of the Birlings and Gerald Croft seem much more callous and morally wrong.

Edna

Edna is an undeveloped character who is present to fulfil the mechanical functions which move the play along such as opening the door and announcing people. Through the very fact that her character is not developed, she does also serve as an extra emphasis of how the servant class were seen by their rich masters.

Add your own notes here:

What is the significance of when the play is set?

Although first performed in 1946, "An Inspector Calls" is actually set in 1912. This is significant as it was a time when Britain had come through the long Victorian period followed by the relatively short Edwardian period. The class system was thriving in Britain and the country was prosperous. Working people were basically at the mercy of their wealthy masters – in short, an ideal time for the proliferation of people such as Arthur Birling. By using this era as a setting, Priestley was able to starkly portray the polarisation of class division with its associated injustice far more easily than a play set in 1946 could have. This, you could say, was the heyday of the class system before it was eroded by the trials of the First World War and the Great Depression.

In addition, by setting the play just before some of the famous events of the twentieth century such as the sinking of Titanic and the First World War, Priestley were able to add to the portrayal of Arthur Birling as ignorant and out of touch when he makes his speech early on.

What is the significance of where the play is set?

The play is set in two rooms of the Birlings' house in Brumley where they are isolated and insulated from the real world around them. It is the population of the real world around them that is affected by their selfish actions but, until the Inspector's arrival, they haven't had to face any responsibility for their actions. The Inspector breaks into their protective bubble and forces them to face up to their actions with varying degrees of success.

Writing about the play

Model introductions for essays

Obviously, each introduction will be different depending upon the essay question it relates to. However, it is possible to prepare general introductions which can be tweaked to link to the particular question. The model introduction below is tailored to a question about characters but can be adapted by changing the linking sentences at the end (the final two sentences of the introduction).

J.B Priestley wrote his play "An Inspector Calls" with the aim of making his audience think about the injustices of the British social system. He addressed themes through the characters he created and he used his audience's relationship with the characters to educate them as to his intentions. In this way, Priestley shows us his interpretation of the evils of rampant capitalism through our perception of the obnoxious Arthur Birling whilst at the same time he gives us some hope of future relief through Sheila's growing realisation of her responsibility for her actions. The Inspector's visit turned the Birlings' comfortable life upside down by making them confront their responsibilities for their behaviour. *The difference was that characters like Sheila and Eric actually learned from the experience whilst Birling patently did not. For these reasons, it is interesting to consider what effect, if any, the Inspector's visit had upon Arthur Birling and Sheila Birling.*

"An Inspector Calls" Practice Essay

Essay: Choose two characters from the play and show what effect the Inspector's visit had upon them.

Introduction:

Briefly say what you think J. B. Priestley was trying to make his audience think about
Briefly set the scene including historical context
Explain the two characters you have chosen and why

A model introduction to this essay:

J.B Priestley wrote his play "An Inspector Calls" with the aim of making his audience think about the injustices of the British social system. He addressed themes through the characters he created and he used his audience's relationship with the characters to educate them as to his intentions. In this way, Priestley shows us his interpretation of the evils of rampant capitalism through our perception of the obnoxious Arthur Birling whilst at the same time he gives us some hope of future relief through Sheila's growing realisation of her responsibility for her actions. The Inspector's visit turned the Birlings' comfortable life upside down by making them confront their responsibilities for their behaviour. The difference was that characters like Sheila and Eric actually learned from the experience whilst Birling patently did not. For these reasons, it is interesting to consider what effect, if any, the Inspector's visit had upon Arthur Birling and Sheila Birling.

Body of the essay:

Deal with each character separately. **Use quotes as your evidence to back up your points**

For each character, keep referring to what you think J. B. Priestley was trying to show through them

- What had they done?
- What was the Inspector's attitude towards them?
- What was their attitude towards the Inspector?
- What were they worried about?
- Were they affected by the Inspector and if so, how?

Then discuss both characters – were either or both of them different at the end of the play than they were at the beginning?

Conclusion:
Sum up your points and conclusions
What does this tell us about J. B. Priestley's aims in writing the play?

Add your own development here:

Some useful targeted quotes

Arthur Birling:

"You'll be marrying at a very good time"

"The Germans don't want war"

"I'm talking as a hard-headed, practical man of business"

"I gather there's a very good chance of a knighthood"

"A man has to mind his own business and look after himself and his own"

"If we were all responsible for everything that happened to everybody we'd had anything to do wit, it would be very awkward"

"There'll be a public scandal – unless we're lucky – and who here will suffer from that more than I will?"

"I'd give thousands –yes – thousands"

Sheila

"If I could help her now, I would"

"I'll never, never do it again to anybody"

"probably, between us, we killed her"

"I had her turned out of a job, I started it"

"I suppose we're all nice people now"

"between us, we drove that girl to commit suicide"

Gerald Croft

"An attractive chap about thirty"

"You seem to be a nice, well behaved family"

"We're respectable citizens and not criminals

"I did keep a girl last summer"

"Everything's all right now"

Sybil Birling

"about fifty, a rather cold woman and her husband's social superior".

"Girls of that class"

"You seem to have made a great impression on this child Inspector".

"You know of course that my husband was Lord Mayor only two years ago and that he's still a magistrate".

"...she had only herself to blame".

"..I accept no blame for it at all".

Eric Birling

"..you're not the kind of father a chap could go to when he's in trouble"

"I'm not likely to forget".

"What does it matter whether they give you a knighthood or not?"

"I say the girl's dead and we all helped to kill her".

Inspector Goole

"He creates at once an impression of massiveness"

"It's my duty to ask questions"

"..it's better to ask for the Earth than to take it".

"Your daughter isn't living on the moon. She's here in Brumley too".

"Each of you helped to kill her".

"Remember what you did".

"...there are millions and millions of Eva Smiths and John Smiths still left with us".

Add your own quotes here:

Finally, it must be emphasised that this booklet is by no means a comprehensive guide to the novel. The aim is to add levels of analysis to a strong foundation of understanding in order to make sure of the higher grades in your end result.

Other guides in this series:

"Of Mice and Men" A* Guide from ACE Notes £1.49

"AQA Anthology 'Conflict' Section" A* Guide from ACE Notes

AQA English G.C.S.E. A* Guide from ACE Notes

"Romeo and Juliet" A* Guide from ACE Notes

All currently available on Kindle and soon to be published in hard copy through Amazon.

Printed in Great Britain
by Amazon.co.uk, Ltd.,
Marston Gate.